S·T·E·M
IS EVERYWHERE!

ROBOTS ALL AROUND US

FROM MEDICINE
TO THE MILITARY

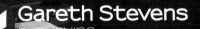

Gareth Stevens
PUBLISHING

EMMETT MARTIN

Please visit our website, www.garethstevens.com.
For a free color catalog of all our high-quality books,
call toll free 1-800-542-2595 or fax 1-877-542-2596.

Portions of this work were originally authored by Ian Chow-Miller and published as *How Robots Work*. All new material in this edition authored by Emmett Martin.

Library of Congress Cataloging-in-Publication Data
Names: Martin, Emmett, author.
Title: Robots all around us : from medicine to the military / Emmett
   Martin.
Description: Buffalo : Gareth Stevens Publishing, [2023] | Series: STEM is
   everywhere! | Includes index.
Identifiers: LCCN 2022022605 (print) | LCCN 2022022606 (ebook) | ISBN
   9781538283530 (library binding) | ISBN 9781538283516 (paperback) | ISBN
   9781538283547 (ebook)
Subjects: LCSH: Robots–Juvenile literature.
Classification: LCC TJ211.2 .M3726 2023 (print) | LCC TJ211.2 (ebook) |
   DDC 629.8/92–dc23/eng/20220706
LC record available at https://lccn.loc.gov/2022022605
LC ebook record available at https://lccn.loc.gov/2022022606

Published in 2023 by
Gareth Stevens Publishing
2544 Clinton Street
Buffalo, NY 14224

Designer: Tanya Dellaccio
Editor: Therese Shea

Photo credits: Series Art Supphachai Salaeman/Shutterstock.com; cover MAD.vertise/Shutterstock.com; p. 5 (bottom) Anton Gvozdikov/Shutterstock.com; p. 5 (top) https://upload.wikimedia.org/wikipedia/commons/8/87/Capek_play.jpg; p. 7 (top) astudio/Shutterstock.com; p. 7 (bottom) Daisy Daisy/Shutterstock.com; p. 9 Engineer studio/Shutterstock.com; p. 11 perfectlab/Shutterstock.com; p. 13 Jenson/Shutterstock.com; p. 14 FeelGoodLuck/Shutterstock.com; p. 15 Suwin/Shutterstock.com; p. 17 (bottom) Gorodenkoff/Shutterstock.com; p. 17 (top) adi_dezt/Shutterstock.com; p. 19 (bottom) Vintage Tone/Shutterstock.com; p. 19 (top) Chaay_Tee/Shutterstock.com; p. 20 Pixel-Shot/Shutterstock.com; p. 21 AlesiaKan/Shutterstock.com; p. 23 Matee Nuserm/Shutterstock.com; p. 25 Gorodenkoff/Shuttertock.com.

Printed in the United States of America

CPSIA compliance information: Batch #CWGS23: For further information contact Gareth Stevens Publishing at 1-800-398-2504.

Find us on

CONTENTS

IS IT A ROBOT?. 4

ALIKE BUT DIFFERENT .6

WHAT CAN IT DO? 8

MORE KINDS OF ROBOTS. 10

THE GOOD AND BAD OF ROBOTS 12

A ROBOT'S PARTS. 16

INSTRUCTIONS 18

OUTPUT, INPUT. 20

ENGINEERING A ROBOT. 24

AMAZING ROBOTS 26

JOIN THE CLUB. 28

GLOSSARY 30

FOR MORE INFORMATION 31

INDEX. 32

Words in the glossary appear in **bold** type
the first time they are used in the text.

IS IT A ROBOT?

Close your eyes and picture a robot. What do you imagine? A humanlike figure made of metal that can walk? A talking computer? What about a dishwasher or toaster in your house? Are these *all* robots?

A robot is different from a machine. A machine is a tool with moving parts that work together. It's made to do something the same way every single time. A robot has moving parts, but it can be programmed to do new things in different ways, often taking the place of a human. This is just one explanation, though. The definition of a robot often changes depending on who's giving it!

WHAT'S IN A NAME?

THE WORD "ROBOT" IS JUST OVER A HUNDRED YEARS OLD. IT COMES FROM A 1920 PLAY WRITTEN BY KAREL ČAPEK CALLED *R.U.R.* (ROSSUM'S UNIVERSAL ROBOTS). ČAPEK USED THE TERM "ROBOT," WHICH COMES FROM THE CZECH WORD *ROBOTA*, MEANING "FORCED WORK." THE PLAY WAS ABOUT A SCIENTIST WHO INVENTS HUMANLIKE MACHINES.

YOUR COMPUTER CAN BE PROGRAMMED TO DO DIFFERENT THINGS, BUT IT DOESN'T HAVE PARTS THAT HELP IT DO HUMANLIKE TASKS. A ROBOT THAT LOOKS HUMAN, LIKE THIS, IS CALLED A HUMANOID ROBOT.

ALIKE BUT DIFFERENT

Like machines, robots need power to work and move their parts. A robot usually runs on electricity, whether it has to be plugged in or is powered by a battery. A fully powered robot can continue to do its job **indefinitely**.

A robot also needs to be programmable. That means you can tell it what to do by pushing a few buttons or writing **code** for it. You can program it and then reprogram it to carry out new actions. While it's possible a machine might do more than one task, it's not made to do anything outside of these tasks.

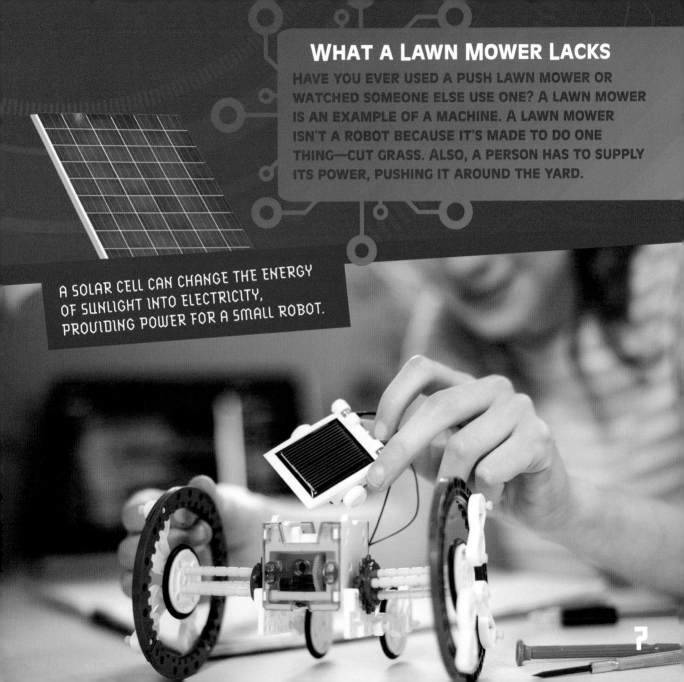

WHAT A LAWN MOWER LACKS

HAVE YOU EVER USED A PUSH LAWN MOWER OR WATCHED SOMEONE ELSE USE ONE? A LAWN MOWER IS AN EXAMPLE OF A MACHINE. A LAWN MOWER ISN'T A ROBOT BECAUSE IT'S MADE TO DO ONE THING—CUT GRASS. ALSO, A PERSON HAS TO SUPPLY ITS POWER, PUSHING IT AROUND THE YARD.

A SOLAR CELL CAN CHANGE THE ENERGY OF SUNLIGHT INTO ELECTRICITY, PROVIDING POWER FOR A SMALL ROBOT.

WHAT CAN IT DO?

What does it mean that a robot can do different tasks without aid? Here's an example: Search-and-rescue robots are programmed to go into damaged buildings after an **earthquake** and locate people trapped inside. The robots don't need help finding the people besides their programming.

THINK BACK

AT THE BEGINNING OF THE BOOK, A QUESTION ASKED IF DISHWASHERS AND TOASTERS COULD BE CONSIDERED ROBOTS. THEY HAVE MANY PARTS. THEY OPERATE BY THEMSELVES AFTER A BUTTON OR TWO ARE PRESSED. HOWEVER, THEY REALLY ONLY DO ONE MAIN JOB AND CAN'T BE REPROGRAMMED, SO THEY AREN'T ROBOTS.

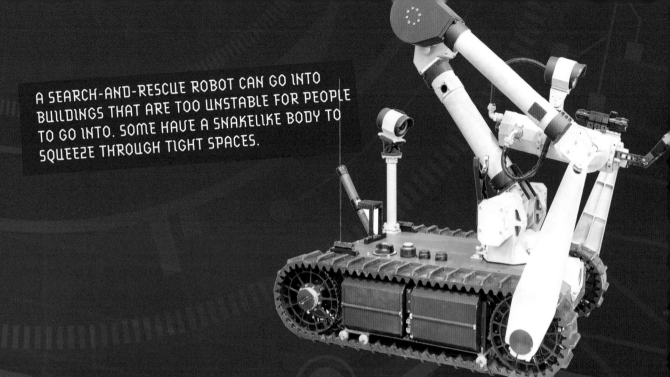

A SEARCH-AND-RESCUE ROBOT CAN GO INTO BUILDINGS THAT ARE TOO UNSTABLE FOR PEOPLE TO GO INTO. SOME HAVE A SNAKELIKE BODY TO SQUEEZE THROUGH TIGHT SPACES.

But the search-and-rescue robots may face new challenges every time they go into a different building. The weather might be rainy one day and sunny on another day. There might still be shaking from the earthquake. The robot might be finding someone or bringing them water and food. Every search and rescue will be a bit different, but the robot can change its actions.

MORE KINDS OF ROBOTS

Search-and-rescue robots are just one kind. Manufacturing robots help build cars, planes, and other **complicated** machines in large factories. Medical robots in hospitals help doctors repair people's hearts and eyes, and perform other risky operations. Some robots are specially built to explore the surface of Mars, while others study the depths of the oceans. Drones are a kind of robotic aircraft. Their flights can be **autonomous** or controlled from the ground. They're used by the military and farmers, and also as toys.

Other robots are simpler. They're found in more and more people's homes. For example, robotic vacuums and mops can help you clean your home.

ROBOT VACUUMS LIKE THIS USE SENSORS THAT WORK A BIT LIKE HUMAN SENSES TO FIGURE OUT WHAT IS DIRT THAT NEEDS TO BE CLEANED AND WHAT IS AN **OBSTACLE** TO AVOID.

ROBOT VACUUMS

A PUSH VACUUM IS AN ELECTRICAL MACHINE THAT NEEDS YOU TO DIRECT IT TO A CERTAIN PLACE TO SUCK UP DIRT AND OTHER UNWANTED MATTER. A ROBOT VACUUM IS AUTONOMOUS. IT'S PROGRAMMED TO MOVE AROUND YOUR HOME, SUCKING UP DIRT. IT WILL CHANGE ITS MOVEMENTS DEPENDING ON THE OBSTACLES IN ITS WAY.

THE GOOD AND BAD OF ROBOTS

Technology can have positive and negative, or harmful, effects. Robotic technology is no different. One of the biggest positive effects is that robots can do jobs that human beings cannot or should not.

You've already read about robots that go into dangerous areas, like a building that fell in an earthquake, and others that go to places that can't support human life—like the ocean floor and other planets. Robots can also work in places that might have gases unsafe to breathe or chemicals unsafe to touch. In these ways, robots can save lives and further our knowledge of places we can't explore ourselves.

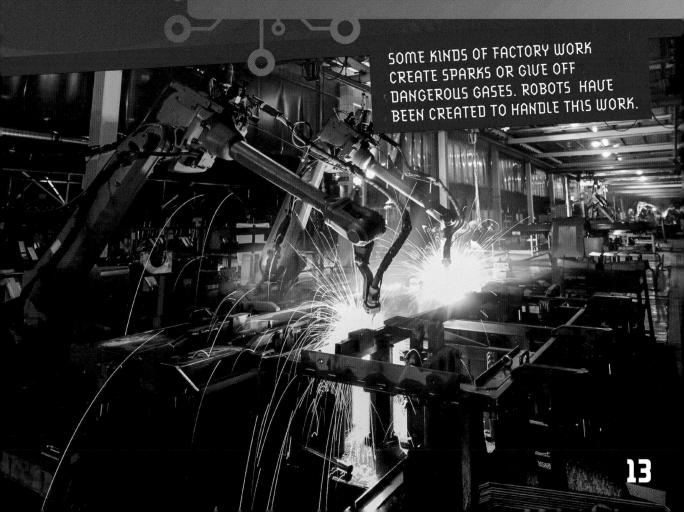

THEY CAN DO THE HEAVY LIFTING

SOME ROBOTS ARE CREATED TO LIFT REALLY HEAVY OBJECTS—LIKE A CAR! OTHERS LIFT LESS WEIGHT, AROUND THE WEIGHT THAT AN ADULT HUMAN MIGHT BE ABLE TO HANDLE. BUT THE ROBOT CAN LIFT IT OVER AND OVER AGAIN WITHOUT THE RISK OF BODILY INJURY THAT PEOPLE FACE WITH EACH LIFT.

SOME KINDS OF FACTORY WORK CREATE SPARKS OR GIVE OFF DANGEROUS GASES. ROBOTS HAVE BEEN CREATED TO HANDLE THIS WORK.

Many people think a negative feature of robot technology is the replacement of human workers. For example, factories employ a lot of people. Because many factories need workers to do things over and over in the same exact manner, they are an ideal setting for robots.

A REAL IMPACT

A MASSACHUSETTS INSTITUTE OF TECHNOLOGY (MIT) PROFESSOR, DARON ACEMOGLU, STUDIED HOW ROBOTS WERE AFFECTING THE U.S. WORKFORCE. HIS RESEARCH, PUBLISHED IN 2020, FOUND THAT EACH ROBOT REPLACED ABOUT 3.3 JOBS. HE ALSO NOTED THAT THE USE OF ROBOTS IN MANUFACTURING HAD A POSITIVE OUTCOME, REDUCING THE COST OF GOODS.

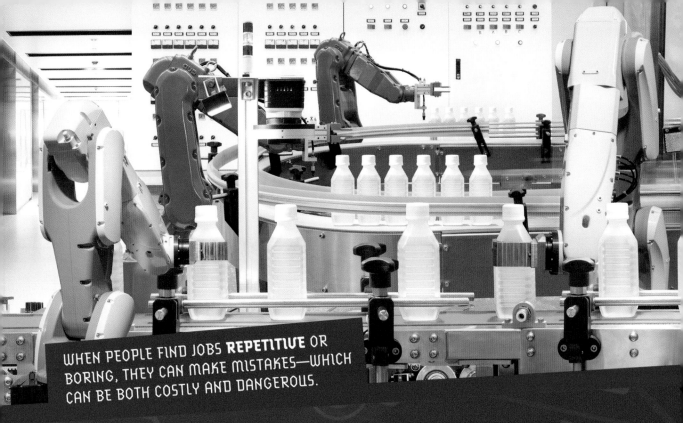

WHEN PEOPLE FIND JOBS **REPETITIVE** OR BORING, THEY CAN MAKE MISTAKES—WHICH CAN BE BOTH COSTLY AND DANGEROUS.

Robots can work in a factory doing the same repetitive job all day long without getting tired. They can even keep working all night. They don't get paid extra. Many people fear that since robots can do the work better, faster, and longer, more and more people will lose their jobs to robots.

A ROBOT'S PARTS

Not many robots actually look like humans, but we can use the human body to help us understand robot parts. A robot has a part called a central processing unit (CPU) that works like a brain. The robot also has parts called sensors that collect information, or data, about its surroundings, a bit like our senses collect data for our brains. The CPU may use this data to begin or end an action, depending on the robot's programming.

The CPU has a power connection point. Wires from sensors and motors also need to be connected to the CPU.

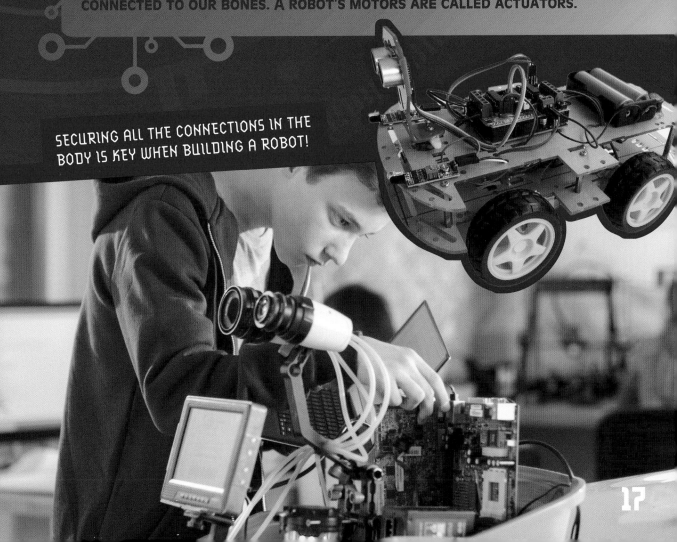

A ROBOT'S "MUSCLES"

WHY DOES A ROBOT NEED MOTORS? SOME ROBOTS HAVE PARTS LIKE ARMS, LEGS, TREADS, AND WHEELS. THEY MAY BE MADE OF METAL OR PLASTIC. FOR THESE PARTS TO MOVE, THEY NEED TO BE CONNECTED TO MOTORS, LIKE MUSCLES ARE CONNECTED TO OUR BONES. A ROBOT'S MOTORS ARE CALLED ACTUATORS.

SECURING ALL THE CONNECTIONS IN THE BODY IS KEY WHEN BUILDING A ROBOT!

INSTRUCTIONS

What do you do when you're hungry? You might make a sandwich to solve this problem! You follow a few steps: First, take out bread. Then, choose the other ingredients. You might place them in a certain order. If you don't have one thing, you might not include another.

An algorithm is the word for a list of steps to solve a problem. When a programmer wants to give a robot instructions, they create an algorithm. The programmer turns it into code using a computer language the robot understands. Different robots use different computer languages, so the programmer must be familiar with the right language.

NOT-SO-SECRET CODES

NO ROBOT HAS A BRAIN THAT THINKS IN A COMPLICATED WAY LIKE A HUMAN'S DOES—AT LEAST NOT YET! A PROGRAMMER USES THEIR OWN BRAIN TO WRITE CODE FOR THE ROBOT'S CPU. THIS CODE TELLS THE ROBOT WHAT TO DO, LIKE HOW TO GATHER DATA AND WHAT TO DO AFTER RECEIVING THAT DATA.

THE STEPS OF AN ALGORITHM ARE FOLLOWED IN A CERTAIN ORDER TO SOLVE A PROBLEM OR PERFORM A TASK. AS CODE, IT MIGHT LOOK LIKE THIS.

```
if not os.path.
#Call function to generate
if(item_Event == "RT_EVENT")
if(item_Event == "RT_CHAIN
if(item_E
```

OUTPUT, INPUT

A robot's CPU reads the code the programmer gives it. Then, it follows the code's instructions. These instructions could be to turn on a motor, flash a light, or honk a horn. Whatever the action is, there must be a robot part to carry out that action. These parts are called outputs because information is sent out from the CPU to them.

END EFFECTORS

SOME ROBOTIC ARMS HAVE PARTS ON THEIR ENDS THAT CAN BE CHANGED, MAKING THE ROBOT EVEN MORE USEFUL. FOR EXAMPLE, IN A FACTORY, A ROBOTIC ARM MIGHT END WITH A WELDING TOOL THAT CAN BE CHANGED INTO A PAINT SPRAYER. THESE ARM ENDS ARE SOMETIMES CALLED END EFFECTORS.

A common type of output on a robot is a motor. The motor, when supplied with power, provides movement to a part. A motor can connect to a wheel or track for movement. It can also connect to an arm for lifting, grabbing, or pushing.

The opposite of outputs are inputs. Inputs are how the robot takes data into its CPU, which allows it to change its actions if it has code that directs it to change. Sensors are inputs made to collect a certain kind of information. Then, they send the information to the CPU. The CPU makes decisions, but again, only according to its programming.

INPUT AT WORK

ROBOT VACUUMS USE A SENSOR TO MEASURE CHANGES IN LIGHT AROUND THEM. THEY SEND THESE MEASUREMENTS TO THEIR CPU. THE CPU HAS A CODE THAT TELLS IT WHEN A CERTAIN LIGHT MEASUREMENT MEANS AN OBJECT IS IN THE ROBOT'S WAY. THE ROBOT WILL THEN MOVE TO AVOID THE OBSTACLE.

THIS ROBOT HAS SENSORS IN THE FRONT THAT ALLOW IT TO FOLLOW A LINE.

There are many types of sensors possible in a robot, though not all robots have them. Some sensor types detect color, sound, light, and temperature. Sensors are similar to senses that humans have, like the ability to see, hear, feel, and even taste.

ENGINEERING A ROBOT

Engineering means planning and making structures, products, or systems using science. You know about engineering if you've ever built a fort that fell over and then rebuilt it more successfully using what you learned from your mistake.

Mechanical engineering is the kind that has to do with designing and building machines—and robots. Electrical engineers can apply their knowledge to the electrical systems that would supply the power to a robot, including its CPU. And computer scientists work on "the brain" of the robots and the programs that tell them what to do. Some schools have a robotics degree that combines these courses of study.

SOMEONE WHO WORKS IN ROBOTICS IS CALLED A ROBOTICIST.

WANTED: CAREFUL CODER

NO MATTER HOW WELL ENGINEERED A ROBOT IS, IT WILL GO INTO A WALL OR FALL DOWNSTAIRS, EVEN IF ITS SENSORS SEE THE WALL OR STAIRS, UNLESS IT'S PROGRAMMED TO STOP OR TURN. ROBOTS NEED TO BE TOLD EXACTLY WHAT TO DO, STEP BY STEP.

AMAZING ROBOTS

More and more developments are advancing the field of robotics today. A company called Boston Dynamics makes animal-like robots that walk on all four legs. Their Cheetah robot runs as fast as 29 miles (47 km) per hour. Another, WildCat, can run over all kinds of ground.

Stanford University engineers designed a device that acts like bird claws. When attached to drones, the device allows them to hold onto tree branches and "rest," saving power.

A scientist at Japan's National Institute of Advanced Industrial Science and Technology developed a companion robot. The PARO robot looks like a seal and is meant to provide comfort to hospital patients and others.

ROBOTS ARE CHANGING THE WORLD

MEDICAL

ACT AS SKELETONS TO HELP MOVE HUMAN LIMBS

DRONES

TAKE PHOTOS AND TRANSPORT GOODS

MILITARY

OBSERVE ENEMY FORCES AND FIRE WEAPONS IN COMBAT

SERVICE

ACT AS SERVERS AT RESTAURANTS

EXPLORATION

MAP THE OCEAN FLOOR

EMERGENCY RESPONSE

HANDLE EXPLOSIVES

MANUFACTURING

LOCATE AND TRANSPORT HEAVY LOADS IN WAREHOUSES

HERE ARE SOME DUTIES ROBOTS ARE CARRYING OUT TODAY. THE FUTURE OF ROBOTICS IS ONLY LIMITED BY ENGINEERS' IMAGINATIONS!

BACK TO THE LAB

BOSTON DYNAMICS CREATED THE LEGGED SQUAD SUPPORT SYSTEM (LS3) TO CARRY UP TO 400 POUNDS (180 KG). THE LS3 WAS MEANT TO BE A MILITARY ROBOT THAT COULD MOVE HEAVY LOADS FOR U.S. MARINES. HOWEVER, IT WAS FOUND TO BE TOO LOUD TO BE WITH SOLDIERS IN THE FIELD. SIMILAR, QUIETER ROBOTS ARE BEING DEVELOPED, HOWEVER.

JOIN THE CLUB

Robots of all shapes and sizes will continue to become a larger part of our lives. The best way to get a clear understanding of what a robot is and how it works is to make and program one yourself. Some robot kits you can buy have all the necessary parts and instructions.

In addition, many schools and communities have robotics clubs that teach about the basics of robotics and provide parts to put your knowledge into action. Look for a local robotics contest so you can see young roboticists show off their engineering skills—or enter your own robot creation!

ROBOT TIMELINE

GEORGE DEVOL PATENTS THE FIRST PROGRAMMABLE ROBOTIC ARM, LATER CALLED UNIMATE. — 1954

1920 — **THE WORD "ROBOT" IS FIRST USED IN A PLAY CALLED *R.U.R.***

THE VIKING 1 AND 2 SPACE PROBES USE ROBOTIC ARMS. — 1976

1969 — **VICTOR SCHEINMAN CREATES THE STANFORD ARM, WHICH IS THE FIRST SUCCESSFUL ELECTRIC COMPUTER-CONTROLLED ROBOT ARM.**

MACHINES IN A GENERAL MOTORS PLANT USE "MACHINE VISION" FOR THE FIRST TIME. — 1981

1990 — **THE COMPANY IROBOT IS FOUNDED, WORKING AT FIRST ON MILITARY ROBOTS.**

A SIX-LEGGED ROBOT EXPLORES AN ALASKA VOLCANO. — 1994

2000 — **THE HONDA COMPANY INTRODUCES A HUMANOID ROBOT CALLED ASIMO.**

2000 — **THE DA VINCI SURGICAL ROBOT IS APPROVED TO ASSIST IN CERTAIN MEDICAL OPERATIONS.**

IROBOT'S ROOMBA, A ROBOTIC VACUUM, IS INTRODUCED. — 2002

2004 — **THE OPPORTUNITY AND SPIRIT ROVERS LAND ON MARS.**

PARALYZED PATIENTS USE THEIR BRAINS TO CONTROL ROBOTIC ARMS. — 2012

2012 — **THE CHEETAH ROBOT SETS A NEW SPEED RECORD FOR MOVEMENT.**

AN MIT ROBOT SETS A NEW SPEED RECORD FOR SOLVING A RUBIK'S CUBE. — 2018

2021 — **ROBOT TAXIS BEGIN SERVICE IN BEIJING, CHINA.**

A ROBOT CHEF AT THE UNIVERSITY OF CAMBRIDGE IS PROGRAMMED TO "TASTE" FOOD. — 2022

SMARTER, FASTER

HAVE YOU EVER PLAYED WITH A RUBIK'S CUBE? IT'S NOT EASY TO SOLVE. THE FASTEST HUMAN SOLVED IT IN 4.22 SECONDS. BUT ROBOTS HAVE BEEN BUILT THAT CAN SOLVE A RUBIK'S CUBE IN LESS THAN ONE SECOND! BEN KATZ AND JARED DICARLO OF MIT'S BIOMIMETICS LAB BUILT ONE THAT SOLVED THE PUZZLE IN JUST 0.38 SECOND IN 2018.

GLOSSARY

autonomous: Describing something that works on its own, without human aid.

code: Data in the form of a set of letters, numbers, or symbols that a computer is able to read.

complicated: Having many pieces or stages. Also, hard to understand.

earthquake: A shaking of the ground caused by the movement of Earth's crust.

indefinitely: Without a known end.

obstacle: Something that blocks a path.

paralyzed: Unable to move.

probe: A machine that sends data back from space.

repetitive: Doing or happening many times.

research: Studying to find something new.

rover: A wheeled robotic vehicle for exploring the surface of a moon, planet, or other space object.

technology: Using science, engineering, and other industries to invent useful tools or to solve problems. Also a machine, piece of equipment, or method created by technology.

welding: Joining metal parts together by heating.

FOR MORE INFORMATION

BOOKS

Graham, Ian. *You Wouldn't Want to Live Without Robots!* New York, NY: Franklin Watts, 2019.

Hulick, Kathryn. *Medical Robots.* Minneapolis, MN: Core Library, 2019.

Whiting, Jim. *Robots.* Mankato, MN: Creative Education, 2020.

WEBSITES

All About Robotics
easyscienceforkids.com/all-about-robotics/
Check out the interesting Quick Facts on this page.

Robot
kids.britannica.com/kids/article/robot/353723
Read a short explanation of robots as well as some history behind the concept.

Robotics
www.nasa.gov/audience/foreducators/robotics/home/index.html
Learn how robots are making a difference in space exploration.

INDEX

ACTUATORS, 17

ALGORITHMS, 18, 19

ČAPEK, KAREL, 5

CENTRAL PROCESSING UNIT (CPU), 16, 19, 20, 22, 24

CHEETAH, 26, 29

CODE, 6, 18, 19, 20, 22, 25

DEFINITION, 4

DRONES, 10, 26, 27

ELECTRICITY, 6, 7

EMERGENCY, 27

END EFFECTORS, 20

ENGINEERING, 24

EXPLORATION, 10, 12, 27, 29

HUMANOIDS, 5, 29

INPUTS, 22

LS3, 27

MANUFACTURING, 10, 13, 14, 15, 20, 27, 29

MEDICAL, 10, 27, 29

MILITARY, 10, 27, 29

MOTORS, 16, 17, 20, 21

OUTPUTS, 20, 21, 22

PARO, 26

ROBOT VACUUMS, 11, 22, 29

R.U.R., 5, 29

SENSORS, 11, 16, 22, 23, 25

WILDCAT, 26